from **Pluckley Railway Station**

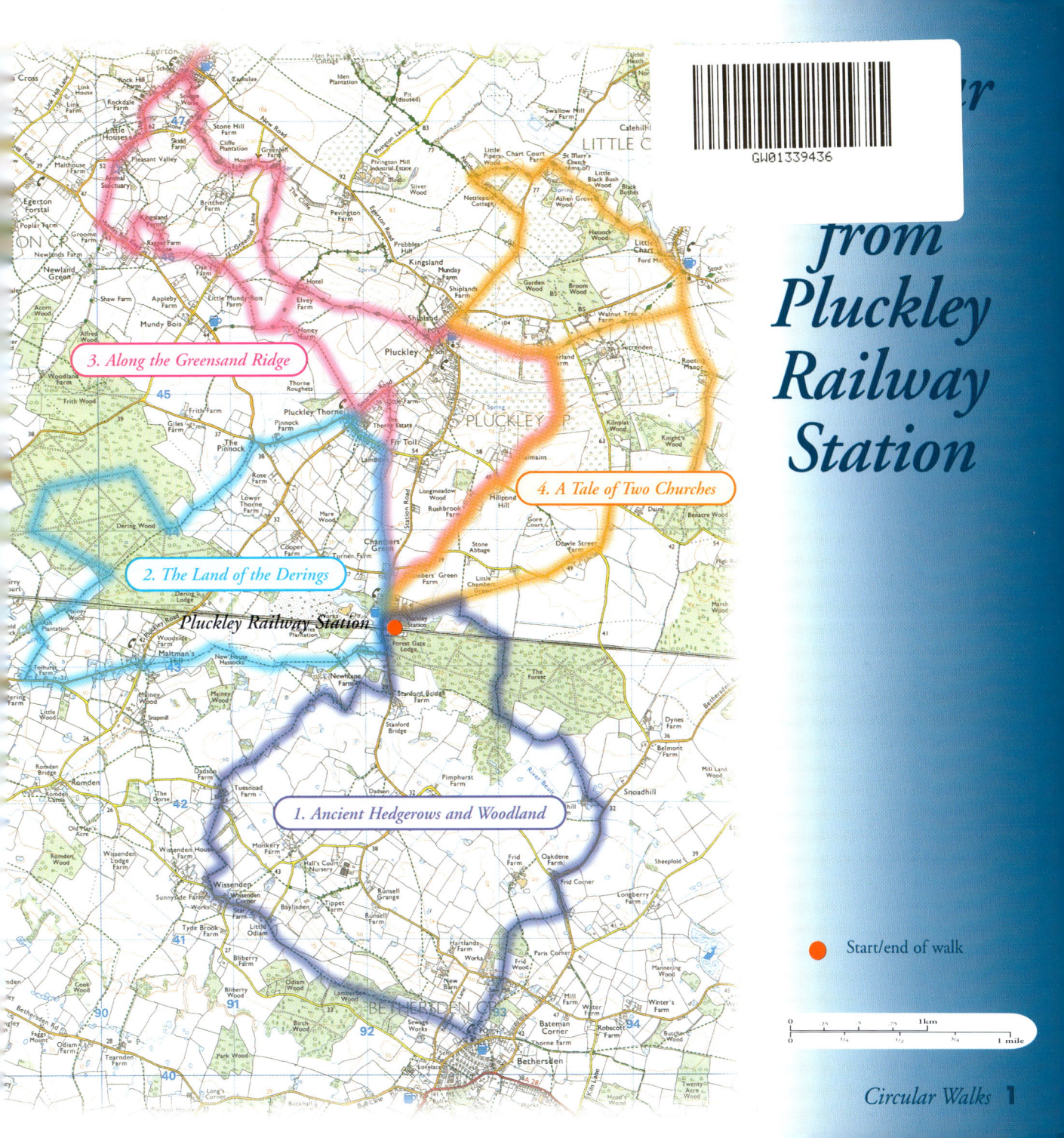

1. Ancient Hedgerows and Woodland
2. The Land of the Derings
3. Along the Greensand Ridge
4. A Tale of Two Churches

● Start/end of walk

Circular Walks **1**

Introduction

The trails pass through villages of the Low Weald and Greensand Ridge with landscapes characteristic of the clay and sandy soils.

Pastures and hay meadows on the neutral clay soil of the Low Weald, where they have not fallen foul of modern agricultural methods, are still full of wild flowers that were once so abundant.

The soil allows farmers to provide ponds as the clay holds water easily, many of these ponds are no longer used to water livestock and so their existence is threatened.

Many old hedges and ditches are still in evidence showing us how the pasture was divided up in days gone by. Woodlands are still managed by coppicing and this encourages a variety of wildlife. Old orchards exist both on the Weald and on the Greensand Ridge but most of these are no longer economic and, like many of the hedgerows, are being left unmanaged.

The Greensand Ridge has a long history of occupation from the Neolithic through the Roman to the Jutish period. The latter gave us place name endings, such as 'den' - a woodland swine pasture.

Most of the area was once owned by the Dering family of the Surrenden Estate and their legacy is to be found almost everywhere. Many of the older and some of the modern buildings have Dering windows and the family emblem of a prancing black horse is still in evidence.

The area is crossed by two recreational walking routes - the Greensand Way, from which there are excellent views, and the Stour Valley Walk. Two of the trails take advantage of these well used rights of way, but most of the time the trails follow lesser known paths that show the full beauty and range of the countryside of this part of Kent.

Acknowledgments

Bethersden Parish Council
Egerton Parish Council
South of England Rare Breeds Centre
The Woodland Trust

Le chemin de randonnée traverse plusieurs villages et permet d'observer les paysages campagnards typiques des sols argileux et sableux de la région.

Les prairies et les pâturages qui reposent sur le sol argileux et neutre du Low Weald (pour ceux qui ne sont pas tombés dans l'engrenage des méthodes agriculturales modernes, peu respectueuses de la biodiversité), recèlent encore aujourd'hui toute une myriade de ces fleurs sauvages qui autrefois étaient abondantes partout.

Les sols du Low Weald, de part leur nature argileuse qui facilite la rétention d'eau, ont permis autrefois aux fermiers de disposer de nombreuses mares et étangs. Cependant, la plupart de ces points d'eau n'ayant plus à l'heure actuelle vocation à être utilisés en tant que réservoir d'eau pour le bétail, leur existence est désormais menacée.

Beaucoup de vieilles haies et fossés sont encore bien visibles, preuves vivantes s'il en faut de la façon dont furent divisés les pâturages par le passé. Les bois traversés témoignent encore quant à eux d'une gestion forestière traditionnelle en taillis, qui favorise la vie sauvage que l'on y rencontre.

Au niveau du Weald et du Greensand Ridge, on peut aussi admirer de vieux vergers, mais la plupart ne sont pas rentables économiquement. C'est la raison pour laquelle nombre d'entre eux ne sont plus entretenus à l'heure actuelle, à l'instar des haies.

Le Greensand Ridge a connu une longue période d'occupation depuis le Néolithique, en passant par la période Romaine, puis celle des Jutes, dont dérivent de nombreuses terminaisons de noms de lieux.

La plus grande partie de cette région fut jadis propriété de la famille Dering, originaire des terres du Surrenden, et l'on peut encore apercevoir en de nombreux endroits des traces de cet héritage historique. De nombreux bâtiments anciens et quelques constructions plus récentes portent ainsi la marque des Dering sur leurs fenêtres: l'emblème de la famille, représenté par un fringant cheval noir, est ainsi encore largement utilisé.

La contrée est traversée par deux itinéraires forts plaisants : le Greensand Way, duquel on a d'admirables vues sur la vallée, et le Stour Valley Walk. Deux des chemins de randonnée proposés ici suivent ces itinéraires bien fréquentés, mais la plupart du temps il s'agit de sentiers moins connus permettant d'admirer dans toute sa splendeur la campagne de cette partie du Kent.

1. Ancient Hedgerows and Woodland

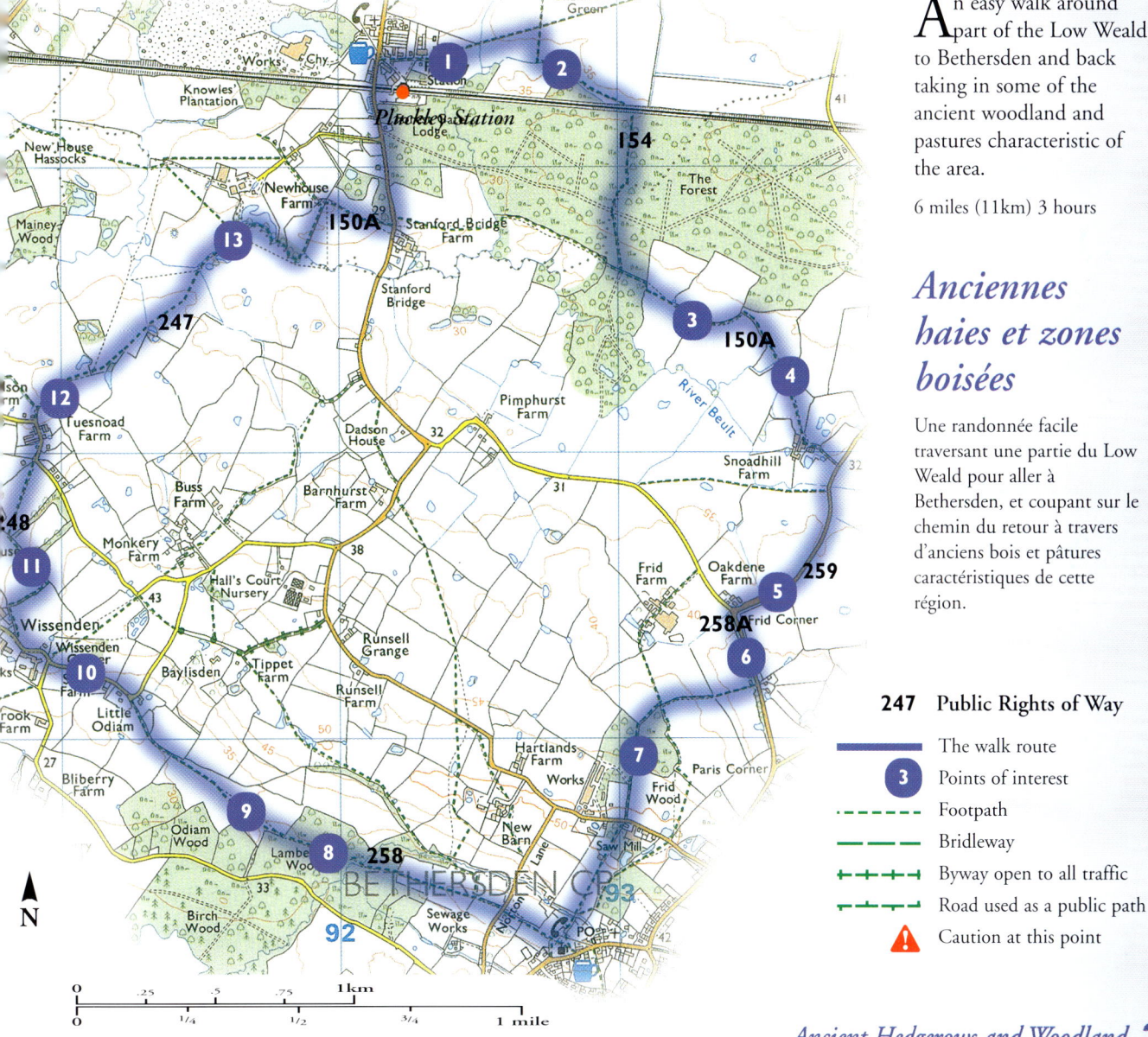

An easy walk around part of the Low Weald to Bethersden and back taking in some of the ancient woodland and pastures characteristic of the area.

6 miles (11km) 3 hours

Anciennes haies et zones boisées

Une randonnée facile traversant une partie du Low Weald pour aller à Bethersden, et coupant sur le chemin du retour à travers d'anciens bois et pâtures caractéristiques de cette région.

247 Public Rights of Way
— The walk route
3 Points of interest
- - - Footpath
— — Bridleway
+-+-+ Byway open to all traffic
-|-|- Road used as a public path
⚠ Caution at this point

Ancient Hedgerows and Woodland **3**

From the station turn left through the car park towards the road. Turn sharp right just before the Dering Arms Pub, along FP 151.

The pub is named after one of the most prominent families of the district. The Derings lived at Surrenden, between Pluckley and Little Chart, for over thirty generations from before the Norman conquest until 1928. The pub has the characteristic "lucky Dering windows" of the area, shaped like an upside down letter U. The local abundance of this design of window stems from the English Civil War. In 1642 Sir Edward Dering fought on the side of King Charles. Cromwell's troops exacted their revenge by sacking Surrenden, but a family member was able to escape through one of these windows. In the 19th century Sir Edward Cholmeley Dering, deeming that this pattern of window brought luck to the family, had all the windows in the estate changed to this style.

Go through the metal gate at the end of the track, cross the garden and enter the field using the stile.

The small meadow **1** contains a marvellous community of plants, black knapweed and tufted vetch (Centaurea nigra and Vicia cracca) being two of the most apparent in high summer. This mass of flowers supports an abundance of invertebrates. Numerous butterflies abound and the grass is noisy with grasshoppers.

Go diagonally left through the meadow to cross a stile between two oaks. Continue in the same direction until just after the telegraph pole, turn sharp right, now FP 154. Head towards the first oak. On reaching the ditch turn left to skirt the wood.

Although often dry in the summer, the ditch **2** still contains some plants that are indicators of wet ground. Hemlock water-dropwort (Oenanthe crocata) is probably the most noticeable and, scrambling through the tall vegetation, is bittersweet (Solanum dulcamara). This plant belongs to the same family as tomatoes and potatoes and the relationship can easily be seen by looking at the flowers. In this case they have blue petals with a yellow cone but are the same shape as those familiar garden plants. It is mistakenly called "deadly nightshade". Although of the same family as that truly deadly plant, it is one of the less poisonous members. The bright red berries at first have an intense bitterness, followed by a sweet after-taste, hence the name. Do not test this as they are a strong purgative and the nearest lavatory is in the station! The leaves, if crushed, have a strong smell of burnt rubber.

Climb the ladder stile and carefully cross the railway into the wood and follow the path.

This wood is called The Forest and has the usual mixture of trees indicative of the clay soil of the Low Weald - large English and sessile oaks (Quercus robur and petraea) with an understorey of coppice hornbeam (Carpinus betulus). The track edges also exhibit some of the plants regularly found on this soil type. Foxglove and goldenrod (Digitalis purpurea and Solidago virgaurea) occur in profusion. In sunny spots musk mallow (Malva moschata) may also be found.

Carry straight on over the cross road.

There are a number of horse chestnuts (Aesculus hippocastanum). This well-known source of conkers is now considered an "honorary native" tree, but is truly native to the Balkans. The seed was brought to northern Europe from Constantinople by the botanist Charles de l'Ecluse in 1576. The derivation of the name is not really known. In its native

Musk mallow

Dering Arms

4   *Ancient Hedgerows and Woodland*

Common blue

Turkey it is given to horses both as food and medicine. Also, when a leaf falls off it leaves behind a horseshoe-shaped scar complete with nail-like marks. Perhaps because of its more southerly origins, it is one of the first large trees to come into leaf in the spring, and the first to turn brown as autumn approaches.

Turn left at the next track onto FP 150A. Exit the wood turning right, then almost immediately left across the field towards the single oak. Continue, keeping the ditch and hedge to the left, through an old gateway towards another stile.

The hay field **3** is not overly improved with fertilizers and pesticides and as such is fairly rich in wildflowers. In the summer most noticeable are the drifts of yellow common bird's-foot-trefoil (Lotus corniculatus). This wide-spread member of the pea family is the preferred food plant of the caterpillars of the common blue butterfly (Polyommatus icarus). This striking blue butterfly has fared much better than many of its more specialised relations, being still widely distributed. Like many well-known plants, this trefoil has attracted over 70 alternative names. In Kent two that are still often used are eggs and bacon, after its flowers, and granny's toenails, after the claw-like seed pods.

Leave the hay field via the stile and turn right along the hedge. As the hedge ends continue through the field and another old gateway, heading for the white farmhouse of Snoadhill Farm.

Although somewhat neglected now, many of the hedges **4** show some sign of having been laid in the past. Before wire fencing, stock-proof hedges were maintained by cutting the upright stems of the shrubs virtually all the way through, then laying the plant over. With each laid on top of the next for the length of the hedge, a barrier was created that even lambs had trouble getting through. Not only did this provide stock proofing, it also prolonged the life of the hedge. It will be noticeable almost throughout the length of the walk the number of hedges that have now become just a series of tall trees. As evidence of laying, look out for trees in the hedgerows, especially hornbeams, with limbs stretching horizontally close to the ground.

Chequer tree - leaves and chequers

Go over the stile opposite the side of the farmhouse. Turn left down the track and right at the road.

Amongst the larger trees on the right **5** is a fine wild service tree (Sorbus torminalis). It is a fairly scarce and certainly over-looked tree these days, but twice a year it is quite stunning - in spring covered in white blossom; in autumn brilliant scarlet, copper-tinged leaves. It is also known as the chequer tree and the Weald has many Chequers pubs. These were not originally named after the board game normally portrayed on their signs, but this tree. The fruit was used to make a drink akin to sloe gin and many pubs kept chequer trees to provide the ingredients.

Ancient Hedgerows and Woodland **5**

Bethersden Church

Go left at the 'T' junction.
At the base of the hedgerow **6** many lords and ladies (Arum maculatum) may be found. This is another plant with a multitude of names, many of them rude after the shape of its flower parts; a long thin spadix partially cloaked in a green sheath. Even its most often used other name – cuckoo-pint – is a corruption of cuckoo's pintle, which was slang for penis. One wonderful, and almost botanically correct one, is willy lily - the plant being a member of the arum lily family. A more prosaic name is starchwort, as the tubers were ground up to provide starch for the laundry industry.

Turn right just past Cloverlea B&B on to FP 259. Cross the arable field, heading first for the gap in the ditch then the right side of the small wood, FP 258A. Carry on down the edge of the wood, finally entering the wood over a stile.

This part of the wood has a plantation of hybrid poplars **7**, which are very fast growing and quickly produce a great deal of timber. It was used to make matches, but has now been usurped by imported softwoods. Its main use today is to provide timber for the production of pallets. In summer the floor of the wood is covered in enchanter's nightshade (Circaea lutetiana), a grand name for this fairly insignificant willowherb, although the tiny pink fringed flowers are worth a closer look. The name may be derived from its tendency to grow in dark, shady woods; another, more fanciful, idea is that it was the charm used by Homer's witch Circe to turn Ulysses' crew into pigs.

Go through a builder's yard, cross the road and enter another stand of poplars via a stile. Continue straight ahead heading for the tower of Bethersden Church. Head towards the church until meeting the path that crosses the churchyard.

For a few centuries Bethersden was famous for its marble. Although not true marble it could be fashioned and polished to appear very similar. Kent's two cathedrals and many of its churches and large houses are embellished with this stone. Strangely, the village's own church only has the south porch paved with marble. However the locals had a much more practical application using it to make causeways across the sticky Wealden clays to aid the passage of pack horses loaded with wool and woollen goods going to the markets that made this area one of the richest in England for four hundred years.

Another of this village's claims to fame is that it was the home of Richard Lovelace, the Cavalier poet. He was the originator of the well known line: "Stone walls do not a prison make" from his poem To Althea, from prison. He wrote the poem during his imprisonment in the gatehouse of Westminster Palace for trying to deliver the Kent Petition to both Houses of Parliament in April 1642. This petition had been drawn up by the county's most prominent families, including the Derings, in the name of the knights, gentry and common people of Kent promoting a "good understanding" between King and Parliament. The hope of this was that law-abiding people could obey the laws of both, and not be forced to cause offence by having to choose between Crown and Constitution. Four months later the Civil War erupted.

The name Bethersden means Beaduric's woodland pasture - Old English Beadurices denn - finally reaching today's spelling in 1610. The "den" ending of place names is very frequent in the Weald and comes from the time when it was very heavily wooded. Livestock, particularly pigs, were allowed to roam the woods in search of food. Now much of this woodland has gone, but its memory is still retained.

Turn right along the path and exit the churchyard via the kissing gate under the large oak. Follow the right-hand

Ancient Hedgerows and Woodland

Old laid hornbeam

edge of the field, FP 258, over another stile until exiting on to the road over a third stile. Cross the road and enter the field through the metal gate. Walk straight ahead to an old gateway then bear slightly left towards an opening in the hedge. Cross directly over the field and enter into the wood over the stile. Follow the track through the wood.

Instantly noticeable is the lack of undergrowth in this wood 8 . It is caused by the dense shade cast by the hornbeam coppice. With very little light penetrating the canopy next to nothing is able to grow, except in early spring before the trees sprout their leaves. One advantage of this is that other features of the woodland floor can be seen. Running almost parallel to the path is a ditch and bank. This is probably a remnant of the time when this wood was wood pasture, with the bank topped with a laid hedge to stop livestock straying. The name - Lamberden Wood - also indicates its past use. This time the name possibly meaning loamy, woodland pasture.

Cross the bridge and continue straight on.

The wood contains areas of cut coppice which show the explosion of growth which occurs once the shade is removed. This is another potentially good place for searching out woodland birds attracted by the increased prospects of finding a meal of insects or seeds in the clearing. One plant that can be found in flower in the densest of shade in this wood is violet helleborine (Epipactis purpurata). The whole plant has a purple tinge to it. This orchid is a fairly rare plant, but in August and early September its clumps of flowers can be found in profusion beside the path.

Leave the wood via the stile and bridge. Walk along the edge of the field until reaching the corner of the wood and then head diagonally right, across the field.

The small pond 9 that is passed is quite a little oasis in this arable desert. Two of the plants that inhabit it are greater reedmace and common water plantain (Typha latifolia and Alisma plantago-aquatica). Reedmace is more commonly known as bulrush. Botanically this is not correct - bulrush (Scirpus lacutris) being a different species. This confusion is thought to have been generated by Sir Lawrence, Alma-Tadema's painting, 'Moses in the Bulrushes', in which the basket containing the baby is clearly depicted hidden amongst reedmace.

Skirt around the pond and go directly across the field. Cross a stile and continue with the hedge on the right. Pass over the next stile, then turn left along the road.

The road verge 10 on the right is rich with plants, including pepper saxifrage (Silaum silaus), an indicator of undisturbed heavy clay soils. It is difficult to find when not in flower, its feathery leaves smell of parsnips when crushed and in the late summer, it is easy to see its clusters of yellowish flowers.

At the road junction turn right towards Smarden. Turn right opposite

Ancient Hedgerows and Woodland

Pepper saxifrage

Sunnyside Farm, onto FP 248. Follow the left-hand edge of the field. Cross the stile in the hedge and turn sharp right again following the hedge line. Do not go through the metal gate, but turn left down the hedge until crossing a stile and bridge through the hedge.

Again, there is ample evidence here of ancient hedge banks [11], these may also be indicators of when the area was completely wooded. The deforestation started as the Saxon swine pastures became settlements and the settlements became villages. When Edward III established Flemish weavers around Cranbrook, the Kentish side of the Weald was transformed. Much of the wood pasture was cleared to create grazing for sheep that provided wool for this new industry, which in turn provided much of the money to fund Edward's war against the French.

Cross diagonally towards the left corner of the field. Turn left at the road. At the waymarker post take the right-hand fork, turning right along the arable field edge. Continue straight on across the field to cross the next stile. Follow the right-hand field edge and cross the small ditch. Cut diagonally across the field, aiming for the small trees just to the right of the large one.

A number of ponds [12] have been passed on the route. Their origin is contentious, it is often said that they were the aftermath of clay workings, ie excavation of the clay to make bricks or pottery. The more likely explanation is that they were simply dug out to provide ponds for the sheep to drink from. Sadly many are now in a poor state. Most are choked with trees, hence very little light reaches the pond surface, so very little is able to grow in them. Exacerbating the problem is the coating of duckweed (Lemna sp.) that most have.

Continue along the trackway, with the large ditch to the left. Do not turn off.

The ditch is in fact the River Beult [13] which eventually joins the Medway. This river was called the "swollen one" in ancient times because of its tendency to flood the flat land it winds through. In spite of it being polluted with nitrates here and to a degree canalised to alleviate the flooding, a few water plants can still be found eg water mint and pink water speedwell (Mentha aquatica and Veronica catenata). In stretches of the stream that are not covered in duckweed, whirligig beetles (Gyrinus natator) can be seen endlessly whizzing round in circles.

Continue with the river to the left past two footbridges. Turn left across the third bridge. Bear left through the poplars to follow the left-hand field edge. Take the stile directly ahead, do not take the stile to the left. The path crosses the field heading towards the buildings. Turn left along the road and head back to the station.

Whirligig beetles

8 *The Land of the Derings*

2. The Land of the Derings

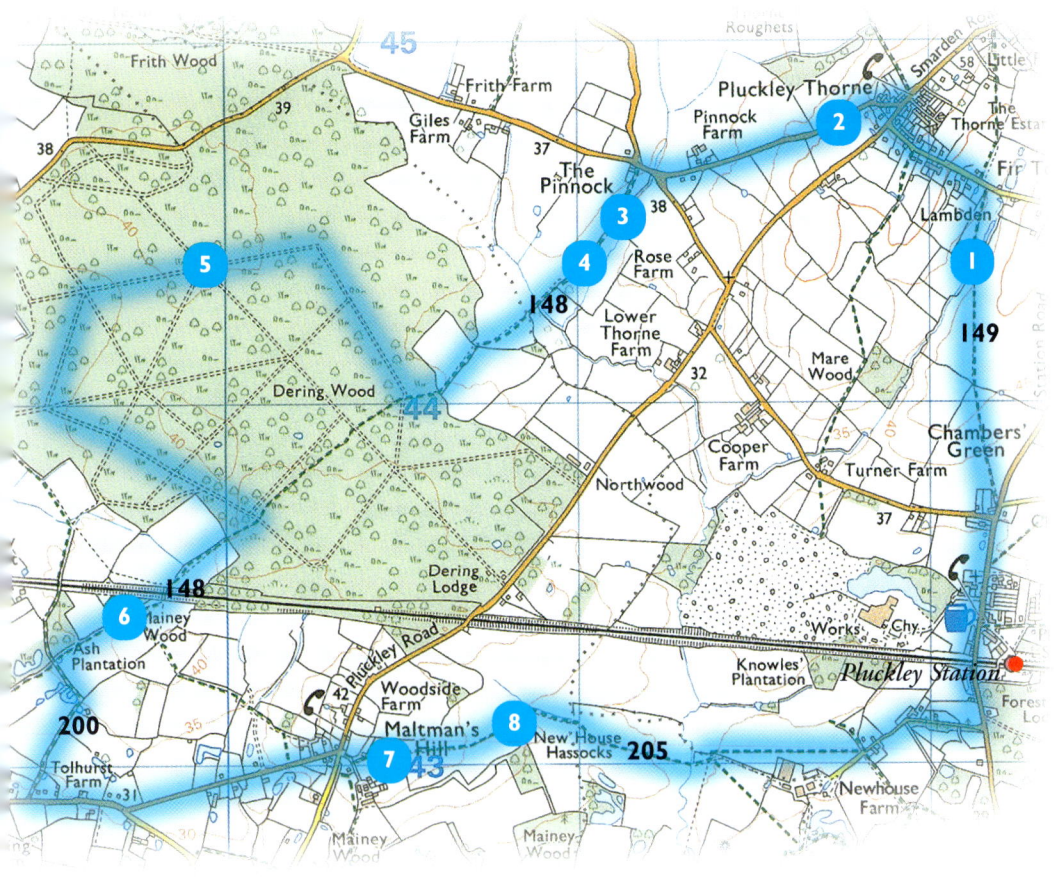

A gentle walk taking in Dering Wood and two other Sites of Nature Conservation Interest.

6 miles (10km) 3 hours.

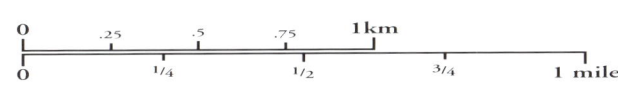

148 Public Rights of Way

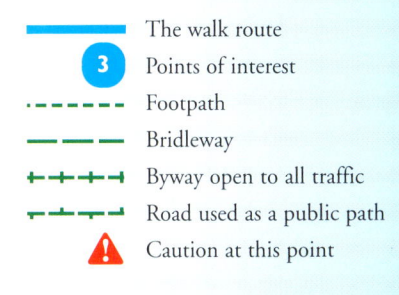

— The walk route
③ Points of interest
- - - - Footpath
— — Bridleway
+++++ Byway open to all traffic
++++ Road used as a public path
⚠ Caution at this point

Les terres des Dering

Une randonnée pour toute la famille passant à travers le Dering Wood, étendue boisée, et deux sites d'intérêt écologique remarquable (Sites of Nature Conservation Interest).

The Land of the Derings 9

Turn right along the road. Continue until just past the road junction to Egerton and Smarden. Take FP 149 opposite the turn to Hothfield. Cross to the left-hand corner of the field. Cross another stile then head diagonally left to another through the hedge, beside the large willow. Cross the stile and bridge.

On the right is a small pond **1**. It has become a little choked with reedmace (Typha latifolia), but is still of some wildlife interest. Around its edge in high summer common fleabane (Pulicaria dysenterica) can be found. This bright yellow daisy is an absolute magnet to nectar feeding insects and any number of butterflies can be seen fighting for a chance to feast from its flower. As the name suggests it was believed that this plant was useful in repelling fleas; with bunches being hung in rooms or dried and burnt in an attempt to fumigate the dwelling. The flower does have an almost antiseptic smell, with hints of carbolic soap.

Cross diagonally to the left-hand corner of the field and turn left onto the road. At the end of Lambden Road turn right then sharp left by the tea-rooms.

On the right is a recently laid hedge **2** and the technique mentioned in walk one is easily seen. Today, hedge-laying is usually done for conservation reasons. It is a hugely labour intensive and time consuming process, with the cut in the bottom of the tree being made with a bill hook - although cheating with chainsaws is now often the case.

When hedge-laying was more common, the layers worked in pairs, preferably one being right-handed and the other left-handed. This meant that a member of the team could work on either side of the hedge; taking alternate cuts at the tree. As the bill hooks were kept razor-sharp, there had to be a great deal of trust between the pair, as one miss-timed cut could cause a lot of damage.

Just past a junction on the left turn left onto FP 148 through a gate, opposite the turning to Mundy Bois and before the house. Follow the hedge on the right to a stile in the right-hand corner of the field.

These two fields **3** have been noted as Sites of Nature Conservation Interest (SNCI). Although a designation with no legal founding it at least means that they have been surveyed and their wildlife interest noted. One of the plants of note recorded from here is yellow-rattle (Rhinanthus minor). This plant is semi-parasitic; acquiring the extra nutrients it requires from the roots of the surrounding grasses. The name derives from the seed pods, shaped like seashells, inside which the seeds rattle when they are ripe.

Cross the stile, continue following the hedge in the same direction.

Hedge-laying

The small pond **4** on the left is a little damaged by the livestock grazing the waterside vegetation and poaching the edges, although they are keeping the water open. One plant they have left is the water-pepper (Polygonum hydropiper), as it has a strong peppery taste. Sometimes the culprits can be seen in the field - British white cattle. These hornless, white animals with black noses and ears are one of the country's prettiest breeds. Although not rare, it is classified as a "minority breed" which means its numbers are not high but not, as yet, in danger of extinction. It comes from East Anglia where it was kept for milk; as more productive milk-producing breeds came along its use changed to beef. It is still used today, mostly in its area of origin, as a cross with

Fleabane

10 *The Land of the Derings*

British white cattle

other breeds in a few beef herds.

Go over the stile just before the right hand corner of the field. Continue between the two fences and then through a field, now with a fence to the right. Eventually turn left over a stile and bridge. Go over a stile and through the gate into Dering Wood.

Dering Wood is designated Semi-Natural Ancient Woodland, which means that it existed before 1600. The wood appears in records dating back one thousand years. As the name implies the wood was once part of the Dering Estate. It remained in their ownership until the 1920s, since then it has had a number of owners. In 1997 308 acres (120 hectares) of Dering Wood were purchased by the Woodland Trust with donations by local people and support from the Heritage Lottery Fund. The Trust now aims to manage the wood using the traditional coppice system around which much of its wildlife has evolved. This will safeguard it as part of the landscape, protect its woodland habitats for the benefit of wildlife and allow the public pedestrian access.

Take the path to the right.

In the spring much of the wood's floor is coated with wood anemones and bluebells (Anemone nemorosa and Hyacinthoides non-scriptus). The delicate white flowers of wood anemones are one of the truest indicators of an ancient woodland site. It very rarely produces fertile seeds, and when it does they do not remain viable for long. Instead it spreads via its roots, but at a very slow rate - no more than two metres per century. So woodland that has a carpet of this flower will probably have been continuously wooded for centuries.

Much of the wood is mature hornbeam coppice. These days it has very few uses and is difficult to market. Although the timber is very hard, the stems always grow with a twist in them, so they are of little use for construction work. Its only uses today are as firewood and charcoal. Traditionally, because of its hardness it was used to make butchers' chopping blocks, mallets, balls and skittles and in the days before cheap steel, it was also fashioned into spokes and cogwheels. The name hornbeam is derived from "horn" meaning hard and "beam" which is Old English for tree.

Take the first major turning on the right.

Eventually a large cross path, known as a ride, will be encountered **5**. This was created in 1998. At first glance it may seem drastic, even damaging, but it will re-colonise very quickly. A network of wide rides is vital to retaining a coppice woodland's diversity. They not only support plant and animal communities of their own, but they also form highways that enable wildlife, particularly invertebrates, to move from areas of maturing coppice to newly cut areas. The recent breakdown of the coppice and ride system of woodland management has caused the decline of a number of species in this country's forests. It is increasingly falling to wildlife organisations such as the Woodland Trust and Kent Wildlife Trust to try and reverse the trend.

Turn left onto this new path. At the next track junction go straight over and turn left almost immediately. The path forks left again but carry straight on.

The path now enters an area where bracken (Pteridium aquilinum) is being kept under control. Although very much part of the natural order in the more open areas within a woodland on acidic soil, this fern does tend to take over, shading out all the ground flora. Most wildlife conservation bodies do try and keep it under control so the wood is as diverse as possible. The process seems to be reaping dividends here as the patches of heather (Calluna vulgaris) are starting to spread. A more insidious problem has been apparent - rhododendrons (Rhododendron ponticum). Although doing much the same as the bracken, this introduced species is certainly not part of the natural order in a British woodland. The feral colonies originate from garden escapes and are proving to be a menace in parts of the

Wood anemone

The Land of the Derings **11**

country with acidic soils. The Woodland Trust will be spending a lot of time and money eradicating it over many years so the native ground flora can reach its true potential.

At the next junction continue straight on through an area of new tree planting and then into older woodland. Turn right at the next junction onto FP 148. Exit the wood. Cross diagonally right over the field. Carefully over the railway. On reaching the meadow turn right along the woodland edge. Go through the gap in the hedge into the next field and carry straight on.

These two meadows **6** form part of Dering Meadows SNCI. At first glance they look somewhat ordinary but a closer inspection can reveal a few gems. As would be expected the classic indicator of heavy clay soil, pepper saxifrage, is present. Also a possibility is green-winged orchid (Orchis morio), an orchid that has become very scarce as grassland such as this is lost. In early summer grass vetchling's (Lathyrus nissolia) small cerise flowers can be found peeping through and as the name suggests, this pea has a resemblance to grass; in fact it is almost impossible to find when not in flower.

Cross the stile in the corner of the meadow and turn immediately left to cross another, onto FP 200. After another stile the path turns right past the ponds and follows the avenue of oaks until it bears left to pass over a stile. Turn left at the road. Follow the road to the second road junction. Take FP 205, up the track opposite, turn left across a stile, just past Kennel's Cottage. Cross the field directly to a stile in the hedge.

In the hedge are a number of damson trees (Prunus domestica insititia) **7**. The lineage of this variety of wild plum (P. domestica) has become very muddled over the centuries. It is a cross of blackthorn (Prunus spinosa) and a sweeter fruited plum introduced from Asia. Whether this was deliberate or an accident is unknown. Damsons have now become very much part of this country's hedgerow flora. A little tart straight from the tree, the fruit can be used for jam and pie fillings. In the past the juice was a source of dye for the cotton and pottery industries.

Go through the hedge and cross the field towards the large oak, then follow the field edge.

Although this is not one of the oldest hedges encountered, it is still very fine with a dense mixture of hazel, hornbeam and field maple (Corylus avellana, Carpinus betulus and Acer campestre) **8**. Hedges have become a conservation icon. Although there are probably bigger issues to tackle, they are of importance both to wildlife and as a landscape feature, and undoubtedly a huge number have been lost in recent years. Apart from the obvious direct loss of habitat, hedges are important as "green corridors". With the fragmentation of wildlife-rich areas by agriculture and development, there is the danger of wildlife populations becoming isolated. Hedges play an important role in keeping some form of link between these areas. Many small mammals, birds and especially invertebrates do not like to cross open expanses of fields or concrete, but they will use hedges as a route to disperse.

As the hedge ends the path bears right to a hedge-topped ditch where it turns left onto a rough farm track. About halfway up the hill go over the stile on the left. Head diagonally right across the field. Skirt around the edge of the next small field. The footpath eventually reaches a gate. Pass through and cross the field diagonally towards the right-hand corner (beware of very friendly Jacob's sheep). Turn left onto the road then at the junction left and head back to the station.

Ride creation

12 *The Land of the Derings*

3. Along the Greensand Ridge

This walk climbs up to Egerton, then returns to the village of Pluckley via the Greensand Ridge.

10 miles (15km) 5 hours or an optional shorter route of 5.5 miles (8km) 2 hours.

En longeant le Greensand Ridge

Cette randonnée grimpe jusqu'à Egerton avant de retourner au village de Pluckley via le Greensand Ridge.

15 km, soit environ 5 heures de balade.

Où 8 km, soit environ 2 heures de balade si l'on opte pour le chemin le plus court.

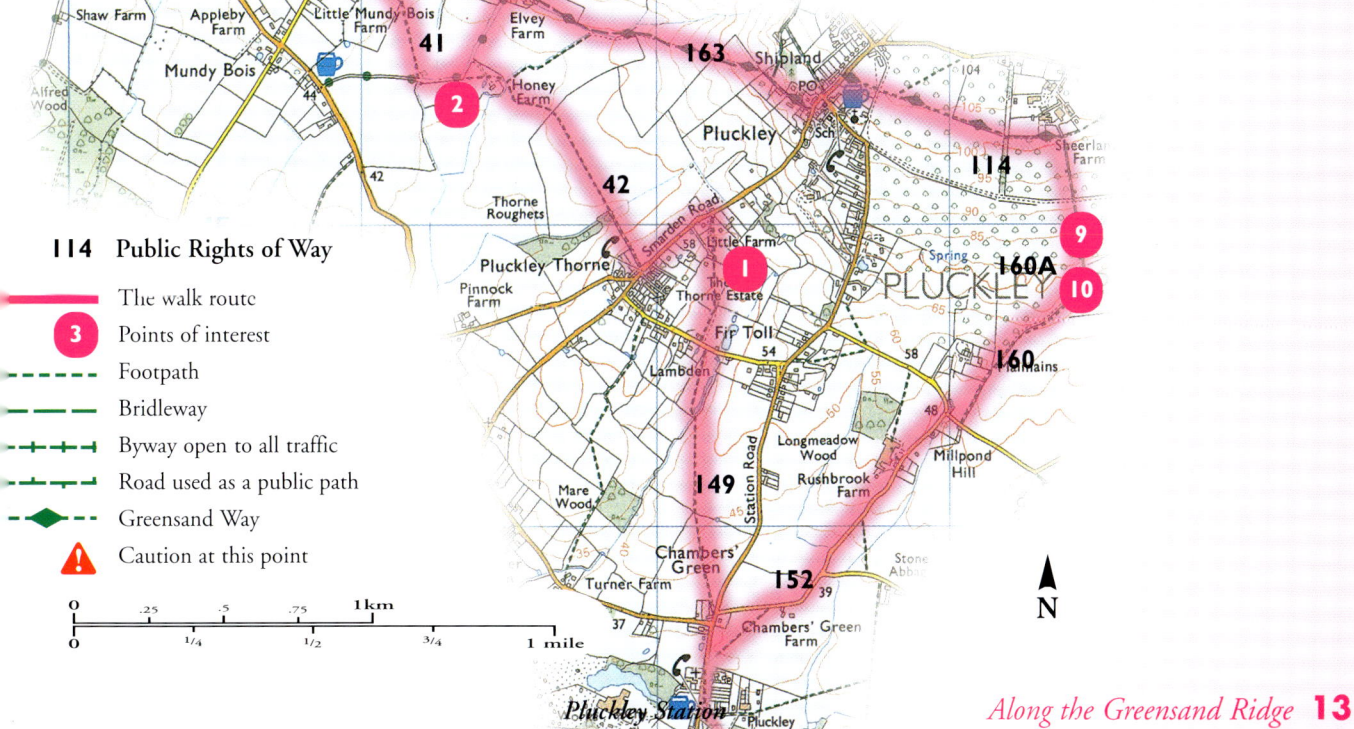

114 Public Rights of Way

— The walk route
3 Points of interest
- - - - Footpath
— — Bridleway
+-+-+ Byway open to all traffic
+-+-+ Road used as a public path
◆—◆ Greensand Way
⚠ Caution at this point

Along the Greensand Ridge

Hedge bindweed

Follow directions for walk two but go over Lambden Road and follow the left-hand field edge before bearing left around a large blackthorn hedge. Cross the field to another stile to the right of the wooden stable.

This horse-grazed paddock **1** although small is very good for plants. Noticeable during the summer are selfheal and red bartsia (Prunella vulgaris and Odontites verna). Red bartsia is semi-parasitic, tapping into the roots of grasses to make up for the lack of nutrients in the soil. It can be quite prolific, being almost the dominant species in the sward. Look out for the short stems of red heather-like flowers.

Cross the track to another stile almost opposite. Cross the field to another stile in the left-hand corner. Go between the garden fences and turn left at the road. Just before the tea rooms turn right onto FP 142. Follow the hedge and then the fence on the left until they end, head across the field aiming for the right side of Honey Farm.

These are not the buildings directly in front but over to the left. Over the stile through the hedge, cross the rough grass diagonally left to another stile, diagonally left again to another stile through a hedge onto the road. Turn left along the road. To take the short cut turn right re-joining the trail at Elvey Farm.

Entwined in the hedge on the left **2** is hedge bindweed (Calystegia sepium). Much hated by gardeners, it is a valuable food plant for hawkmoths. They can hover and probe deep into the trumpet-like flowers with their long tongues to reach the nectar at the base. In fact the largest moth regularly found in this country - convolvulus hawkmoth (Agrius convolvuli) - is entirely dependent on this plant family as it is its caterpillars' only food source.

Cross the bridge over the stream. Turn right into the arable field. Do not go straight across the field but turn left around the edge of the field, eventually crossing a stile in the left corner. Continue along the path between two old hedges, then with a hedge on the right leading to an iron gate. This leads onto the road.

Blackthorn is dominant in the hedge **3** . Its froth of white flowers is one of the heralds of spring as it is usually the first wild tree to flower producing its blooms before it is in leaf. If the weather has been warm, this can be as early as February. It is also the source of the bitter fruit used to make sloe gin which is still produced commercially. It also has some of the sharpest thorns, being capable of puncturing tractor tyres. The hard wood is the traditional material for Irish shillelaghs.

Old pear orchard

Cross the road and turn left. Go over the stile to the left of the first block of houses along the narrow FP 78. Cross a garden to another stile into a field.

These fields **4** have escaped modern agriculture as they are probably too small to be commercially viable. They are used for horse pasture and are crammed with wildflowers. In the summer they are covered in black knapweed and common fleabane (Centaurea nigra and Pulicaria dysenterica) and other nectar rich plants and, because of this, support huge numbers of butterflies and bees.

14 *Along the Greensand Ridge*

Go straight across the pasture to a gap in the hedge and cross a stile. Cross the next field to another stile on the left edge. Cross another field diagonally left to a stile at the left edge of a garden. Go through the pony paddock onto the road. Turn right. Turn left through a small iron gate beside a garage. Follow the hedge on the left to a stile in the left-hand corner of the field. Cross the stile and turn left through the orchard, FP 90.

The orchard **5** contains mostly old pear trees, with the occasional apple and plum. It has become very neglected which is great news for wildlife. Every tree is riddled with birds' nesting holes. Some were made by woodpeckers, some are the product of rot, all are potential nest sites. During the breeding season almost every cavity will have an occupant. Most will contain starlings (Sturnus vulgaris), but others could have green woodpeckers, stock doves or tawny owls (Picus viridis, Columba oenas and Strix aluco). The trees, which may be sixty years old, have many nooks and crannies for invertebrates to hide in and over the decades they have acquired a coating of lichens and mosses. The fallen fruit provides an important food source for mammals and birds building up their fat reserves before the onset of winter.

Old orchards such as this are very scarce these days and, once lost, will not be replaced unless re-planted with wildlife conservation in mind. Modern orchards are fairly sterile. Dwarf trees that are easy to harvest are common now and what was a very important and diverse habitat has virtually disappeared.

Follow the hedge on the left to a stile. Cross diagonally left across the next field to a metal gate. Turn right on the road. Cross the stile opposite a house named the "laurels". Cross the pasture, to another stile, keeping the hedge to the right. Cross another stile then follow the path with the hedge on the left to another stile and then along a path between the houses, turning right onto Rock Hill Road. Take the left fork. On reaching the signpost marked Greensand Way, either continue to visit Egerton, or turn right onto FP 81.

Egerton is situated high on the Greensand Ridge with superb views south and west over the Weald. Looking north and east across Holmsdale the villages of Lenham, Charing and Little Chart can be located by their church towers.

On the road into the village are a number of notable buildings. Rock Hill Farm has an 18th century facade on an earlier house. The two tiered stone outside the farm house is a mounting block; it used to aid riders mounting their horses. Spring and Little Manor Cottages are part of one timber-framed late medieval hall house. The George public house was built in the 17th and 18th centuries.

On the highest point of the village is the Church of St. James, which is 101 metres above sea level. It was rebuilt in the 14th and 15th centuries and restored during Victorian times. Its features of note are the Decorated style west window, a three-tiered chandelier that dates from the early-19th century and a modern alter rail depicting St. Augustine, St. Thomas Becket and other saints.

Now follow the Greensand Way as far as Pluckley. Go to the end of the cul-de-sac. Go down the right side of the furthest right bungalow. Follow the field edge to the right corner of the field. Turn

The Church of St. James

Along the Greensand Ridge **15**

right along the road. Turn left through Stone Hill Farm. Bear right over the stile and down the concrete track.

Now it is possible to see some of the superb views across the Weald **6** . This low-lying area was formed many millions of years ago as the chalk dome that covered most of Kent and Sussex was eroded by rivers and the weather leaving the flat expanse of clay seen today. All that remains of the chalk are the ridges of the North and South Downs.

Between the downs and the Weald is the Greensand Ridge, a high band of faintly-green sandstone that runs in an arc from Folkestone in the east, through Ashford and Sevenoaks to Eastbourne in the west. It is one of the major water-sheds of the area with the Rivers Stour, Medway and Beult all having tributaries that rise below the ridge. For many years there have been quarries in the area. Further west, around Sevenoaks, Kent ragstone is still produced and is still in great demand, especially for the large amount of sea-defence works that is carried out around the Kent coast. In this part of Kent the sandstone is not quite so hard and the quarries mostly produce sand. On the left of this path there are a few rocky out-crops and, in places, the soil profile can be seen.

Pass over the stile beside the gate and follow the left-hand field edge, FP 80. By the metal gate go over a stile and a second into an arable field.

On the bank to the left **7** two common plants can be found - greater burdock and traveller's-joy (Arctium lappa and Clematis vitalba). Burdock is the source of the burrs much hated by dog owners. Supposedly the inventor of Velcro was inspired by the way the hooked bristles of the seed-heads catch onto any rough surface. The flavouring of the fizzy drink "Dandelion and Burdock" used to be made from the roots of these plants. As with the sloes mentioned earlier these are also now imported from eastern Europe.

Continue left around the field boundary to a stile. Go up the steps onto the road and turn right. Go over the stile to the right of the entrance to Greenhill Farm. Go left around the edge of the field and cross two more stiles and a bridge and right towards a waymarker post by a stream. Over the stream turn right again to another stile, on FP 83. Follow the tree-lined stream.

The mix of trees **8** along

The Black Horse, Pluckley

the stream is a haven for a number of bird species. One possibility is long-tailed tit (Aegithalos caudatus). This tiny bird is nearly always encountered in a small flock, moving through the trees in search of its insect prey, all the time calling to one another. It differs from other species of birds in the way it constructs its nest. It is bag-shaped, made deep inside the undergrowth and formed from lichen bound together with spiders' web.

The path eventually reaches a stile. Turn right through a metal gate then immediately left over another stile, FP 140. Continue along the hedge until it ends then cross left over the stile and bridge. Follow the path across the arable field towards Elvey Farm.

Like so many of the farms in the area, Elvey Farm has an oast-house, now part of a hotel. Most of the farms grew a few acres of hops (Humulus lupulus) and had their own kiln and brewery to brew beer for their own consumption. This became the basis of the brewing industry in Kent. Today most of the hop-gardens and breweries have gone, kentish hops having been superseded by cheaper foreign imports. Shepherd Neame in Faversham is the only independent brewery of any size remaining in the county.

Continue straight through the farm to a field gate, BR 163. Cross the field keeping the hedge to the right, to another gate. Then follow the field edge for a short way until coming to a junction of 3 fields. Cross the ditch and turn left, pass through a gate head up the hill aiming for the house. The path bears to the right of the house over a

Along the Greensand Ridge

stile then drops down to a metal gate in the left corner of the field. Go up the track and then turn left onto the road. Continue up the hill. To go to the centre of the village cross the road into the street or, to continue the trail, carry on up the hill.

Many of the older buildings in the village have the "lucky Dering" windows mentioned in walk one. The Black Horse pub is one of them. This seven hundred year old pub is also named after the Dering's family emblem.

The village's main claim to fame is its number of ghosts and it is regularly called "the most haunted village in England". As would be expected, the Derings feature heavily in the ghost stories including the Red Lady, who searches amongst the churchyard gravestones for her child. Others tell of a schoolteacher who hanged himself and a highwayman who was run through by a sword at the appropriately named Fright Corner. There has also been a report of an entire fife and drum band marching through one house, and the furniture in the pub has been said to re-arrange itself.

Carry on a short way up the hill then turn right and cross the playing field into an orchard, FP 114. Continue until a junction in the track just past the buildings of Sheerland Farm. Turn right down the track, BR 160A, leaving the Greensand Way.

The trail passes through an avenue of common limes (Tilia x vulgaris) **9**. This tree is a hybrid of the native small-leaved and large-leaved lime (T. cordata and platyphyllos) and has been widely planted becoming very much part of the landscape, whilst its parents are almost forgotten. Pollen records show that small-leaved lime was once one of the most common trees of the "wildwood", but now it is difficult to find growing wild. It hangs on in the remnants of ancient woods and in hedges that are the "ghosts" of cleared forests. This tree had a number of uses in the past. There is a fibrous layer between the bark and sapwood that was stripped for what was called "bast", which was twisted into rope. Its timber was also prized for wood carving and was the material favoured by the famous wood carver Grinling Gibbons, some of who's work can be seen in St. Paul's Church, Covent Garden where an intricate frieze depicts a wreath of flowers and fruit; some with stalks only a fraction of an inch thick.

The orchard **10** that the trail now passes through is very different from the old pear orchard passed through earlier. It is very intensively managed with any "weeds" sprayed out from around the trees, resulting in very little wildlife. This always seems counter-productive as fruit trees are reliant on insects, especially bees, for pollination, without which the fruit would not form. Once the apple blossom has gone there is little else for the bees to sustain themselves on for the rest of the summer. This self-imposed problem of the farmer is evidenced by the patch of wildflowers he has had to sow beside the bee hives, to the right of the track, to provide the bees with food. Although artificially created, this little patch of flowers contains what have become some of the rarest plants in the countryside. Corncockle, corn marigold and cornflower (Agrostemma githago,

Corncockle

Chrysanthemum segetum and Centaurea cyanus) can all be found here. These annuals were all very common in the arable fields of the past, growing up with the crop each year. With today's farming practice of excluding everything except the desired crops from the fields these species are now virtually extinct in this country.

Continue with the row of poplars to the left, FP 160, bear left out of the orchard, past the big house. Follow the hedge on the right until exiting onto a road. Turn right and at the junction left and follow the road. At the next junction bear right. Before the road joins the main road turn left on FP 152 and cut across the field. Turn left on the road and head to the station.

Along the Greensand Ridge **17**

4. A Tale of Two Churches

A gentle walk to Little Chart through the area that once formed part of the Dering estate at Surrenden and back via the village of Pluckley.

8 miles (12km) or an optional shorter route of 6 miles (9km) 3 hours.

Conte de deux églises

Une randonnée accessible à tous jusqu'à Little Chart, traversant des terres qui autrefois faisaient partie du territoire des Dering à Surrenden. Le retour s'effectue en passant par le village de Pluckley.

12 km, soit environ 4 heures de balade.

Où 9 km, soit environ 3 heures de balade si l'on opte pour le chemin le plus court.

115 Public Rights of Way

— The walk route
3 Points of interest
- - - - Footpath
— — Bridleway
+—+—+ Byway open to all traffic
+—+—+ Road used as a public path
⚠ Caution at this point

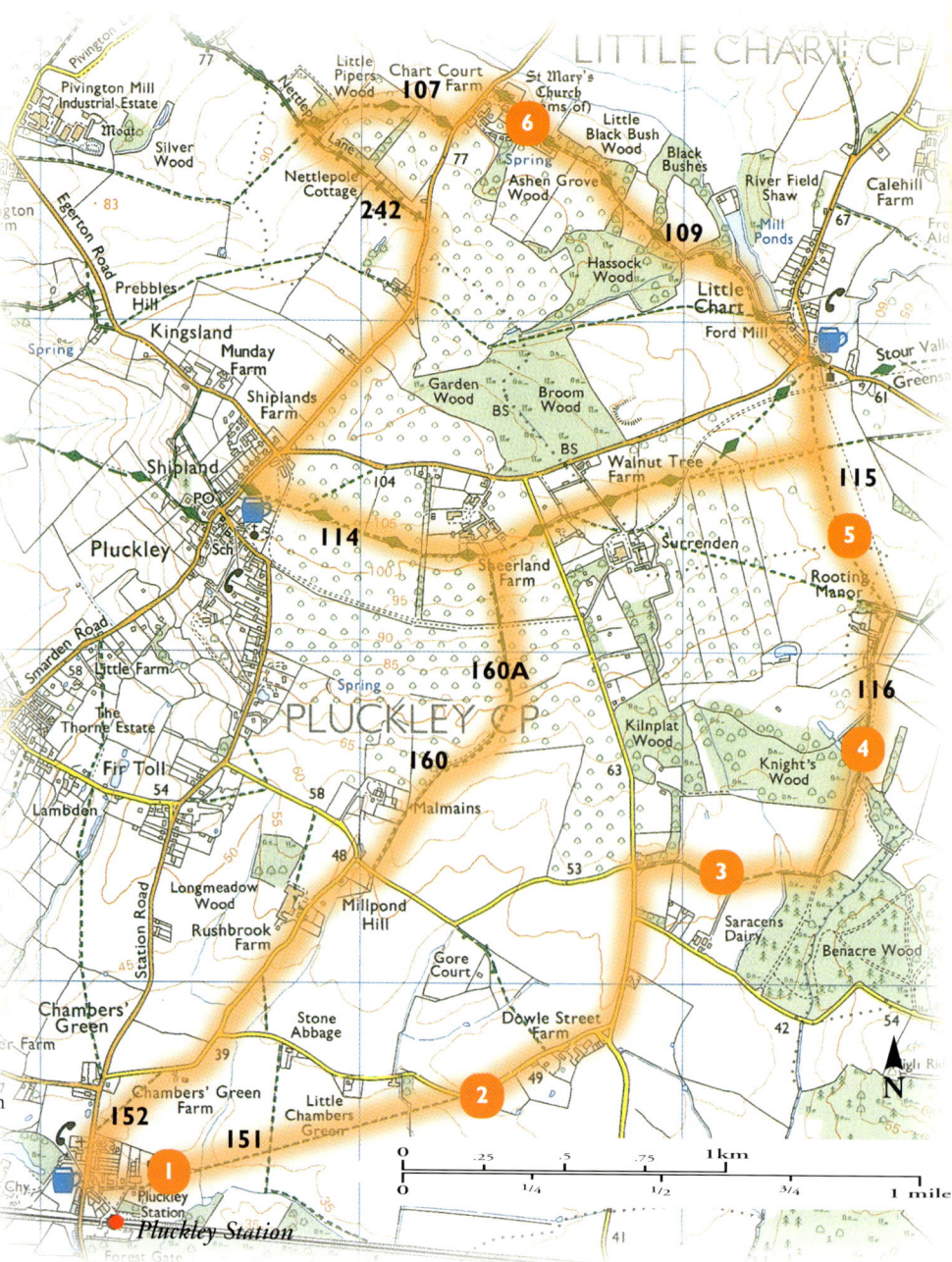

18 *A Tale of Two Churches*

Pollarded oak

From the station car park turn sharp right up the track, FP 151. Pass through the metal gate and cross the garden to a stile. Cross the hay meadow for the oak tree in the left-hand corner. Go over the stile and diagonally left to a bridge and stile through a hedge and continue diagonally left to another stile through a hedge onto the road. Turn right.

For details of the Dering arms pub and the hay meadow **1** see walk one.

In a horse paddock **2** to the right of the road is a huge pollarded oak (Quercus sp.). Pollarding is an ancient form of tree management that involved the regular cutting of a tree's branches about 2 metres from the ground for timber and firewood. In the past many woodlands were grazed, so if a tree was coppiced the stock would eat the re-growth. The remedy for this was pollarding so the new shoots emerged out of reach of browsing animals. Not only did this provide a regular source of timber it also prolonged the life of the tree. Some pollards are centuries old, well beyond their normal life expectancy.

Sadly, these days there is no need for this type of tree management and many old pollards are being lost from the countryside as are the skills needed to carry out the work. These ancient trees are superb wildlife habitats, full of cavities for birds to nest in and for invertebrates to hide in, and are of historical importance as pollarded trees were often used to mark parish boundaries or other places of importance.

Turn right onto BR 116, just before a house named "saracens". After the second gate carry straight on with, at first, a fence on the right and then a wood. Follow the track through the band of woodland and turn left to follow the woodland edge.

Both tawny owl and nuthatch (Strix aluco and Sitta europaea) can be found in this wood **3**. It is unlikely that the owl will be seen although it is not unusual to hear one call. This is the owl that produces the tu-whit, to-woo sound. This call is not made by one owl but two, the first part is by the male and second is the response from his mate.

With a little patience it may be possible to spot a nuthatch. Listen out for their call, a ringing chwit chwit, then look out for a bird with slate blue upper parts and chestnut underside, scurrying up a tree trunk or along a branch. Nuthatches are very woodpecker-like, with their legs positioned towards the back of their body and, with a stout beak, their methods of finding food are similar. Their name is very apt as they have a liking for nuts which they bash open after first wedging them into a crevice. They are also hole nesters, although they do not make their own nest holes but make use of old woodpecker nests. After the female has started to nest the male reduces the size of the entrance with mud, effectively walling his mate in. This deters predators and attempts of take-overs from larger birds such as starlings (Sturnus vulgaris). Once the young are large enough to no longer need incubating the parents remove the mud and the female then joins the male in collecting their food.

The derelict walled garden **4**, and most of the land around once formed part of the Surrenden Estate, the home of the Dering family mentioned in walk one. The wall, built by Sir Edward Dering in the 18th century, is the most impressive remnant of the estate. Although the estate is not recorded as a medieval deer enclosure, up until the 20th century one hundred and fifty fallow deer (Dama dama) used to roam the 350 acre (135 hectares) grounds. The last of the Derings left in 1928 and, after a fire in 1952, all that remains of the house are its lodge cottages.

Follow the road past Rooting Manor to a stile under the fir tree. Cross over and take FP 115 that crosses the field diagonally left towards the new church.

This farmer has provided a decent path over the field **5**. He also does not appear to be too heavy-handed with the use of herbicides. In amongst the redshank and black nightshade (Polygonum persicaria and

Wild pansy

A Tale of Two Churches **19**

Solanum nigrum) growing along the path, field pansies (Viola arvensis) can be found in profusion at almost any time of year. This delicate pale yellow flower is closely related to the gaudy varieties grown in gardens. The wild pansies, such as field pansy and heartsease (V. tricolor) naturally produce a wide range of variants and hybridise very readily. It is these two attributes that plant breeders have exploited to create the huge range of garden varieties that are available.

Exit the field opposite the Swan Inn into the village of Little Chart and turn left along the road and then right onto the signposted 'Stour Valley Walk', FP 109. To take the short cut go left on the Greensand Way until re-joining the trail at Sheerland Farm.

Little Chart developed around a ford across the River Stour. The church was built in 1955 as a replacement for the original one that the trail shortly reaches. The new church has been variously described as "a happy compromise", "strikingly modern" and "heart warming". It contains some relics and treasures retrieved from the older church, including Sir Robert Dering's tomb.

Along the Stour Valley Walk on the right is Ford Mill. This paper mill, along with Chartham Mill, are the only remaining working paper mills left beside the Stour. The first mill on this site was built in 1771. The older buildings were replaced in 1800 by constructions typical of the Industrial Revolution.

Keep the hedge to the right. The trail turns right and then continues with a wood to the left and an orchard to the right. Cross over the stile and continue along the track, passing some farm sheds. Turn right at the junction. Follow the track round then pass between two fences into Little Chart Churchyard.

On the bank **6** at the side of the path are three plants of interest - vervain, soapwort and meadow clary (Verbena officinalis, Saponaria officinalis and Salvia pratensis).

Vervain has tiny lilac flowers that open in succession up the stem until there is just a single one at the tip. In the past this scrawny plant was one of the most revered. It was considered to be a cure for almost any illness, including plague, during the Middle Ages. It was also used as a magic charm, capable of protecting against witches and demons, and conjuring up devilry of its own. Vervain also has a long association with the gods of war. Gun-flints were sometimes boiled with vervain and rue (Ruta graveolens) in the hope that they would become more effective. As with the St. John's wort, the Church absorbed these beliefs by suggesting that it grew under the cross at Calvary. Soapwort may be a native plant but today it is widely planted in the garden, and these are probably garden escapes as the flowers are double petalled. As the name implies, this plant was used as a source of soap. It is rich in saponins, which act like detergent by lubricating and absorbing dirt particles. This plant's properties have been exploited for centuries across Europe and the Middle East. In this country it was used as a soaping agent by medieval fullers. Its long association with washerwomen has led to it acquiring the wonderfully descriptive alternative name of Bouncing Bett.

The ruined church and churchyard are now being maintained by Ashford Borough Council with help from the Kentish Stour Countryside Project as a picnic site. The ruins have been restored enough to make them safe and the graveyard is managed in a way that retains an abandoned look without the site becoming too over-grown.

The church was destroyed by a piece of very bad luck during the Second World War. In August 1944 a Canadian Spitfire pilot successfully intercepted a flying bomb aimed at London. Unfortunately the bomb crashed into the church, demolishing the main body of it. As already mentioned the new church was built in Little Chart; and the people of the village decided to leave the old one as a symbol of the ordeals suffered by Kent in that war.

At the road turn left. After the oast houses carefully cross the road and go through the gate into the orchard, FP 107. Follow the row of poplar trees until a hedgerow comes in from the left. Go through the gateway and bear diagonally left to follow the path through the apple trees. Go over the stile and enter the small wood. On exiting the wood turn left on byway 242, leaving the Stour Valley Walk.

The track is known as Nettlepool Lane and is an ancient route from Stonebridge Green to Little Chart. Its age is demonstrated by the fact that for half its length it has the character of a sunken lane - worn deep into the soft sandy soil by centuries of hoof and foot traffic.

On reaching the road turn right and follow it into Pluckley.

For village details see walk three.

On reaching the village the route back to the station is as walk three.

Bouncing Bett

A Tale of Two Churches